BETWEEN A SILVER SPOON AND THE STRUGGLE

REFLECTIONS ON THE INTERSECTION OF RACISM AND CLASS PRIVILEGE

By Nicole Lewis and Resource Generation

Breaking the silence

—talking about class and coming to terms with where we stand—is a necessary step if we are to live in a world where prosperity and plenty can be shared, where justice can be realized in our public and private lives.

bell hooks

Published by Resource Generation
220 E 23rd Street, Suite 509
New York, NY 10010
www.resourcegeneration.org

Book Design by Seth Gregory
sethgregorydesign.com

Cover texture by 'Playingwithbrushes' on Flickr.
Used under Creative Commons license: Attribution 2.0 Generic (CC BY 2.0)

PRINTED BY CREATE SPACE

Table of Contents

Acknowledgments

Producing this book has been a collaborative effort.

- To everyone who took the time to share their stories with me, many thanks. Thank you for showing your support and excitement for the project by deciding to be part of it!

- Thank you to the Resource Generation staff: Nitika, Jessie, Elspeth, Mike, Sarah A., Sarah S-S, Zara, Isaac, and Tiffany.

- I owe a huge debt of gratitude to Karen Pittelman, who helped to keep me on track with her quirky mix of smarts, humor, and tough love. Thank you.

- To Laura Wernick. Thank you for getting it all started!

- To Seth Gregory for the beautiful design. Thanks for all your amazing work and inspiring brainstorming sessions.

- To the many, many people in my life who have supported me thus far, and who continue to sustain, heal, and challenge me—thank you.

- To the CORE Advisory Committee (Catalyzing Our Resources for Equity)—Anthony Colon, Theo Copley, Molly Hein, Danielle Hicks, Naomi Christine Leapheart, Aya de Leon, Kaberi Banarjee Murthy, Alison Roh Park, Ron Ragin, Darius Ross, Stephan Sastrawidjaja, Monica Simpson, Maxim Thorne, Lloyd Martinez, and Jen Willsea. There would be no book without your insight and vision for RG's work with young people of color with wealth.

- To Dani McClain who got this project off the ground. I could not have completed this book without your efforts. I give thanks to all the people you consulted on this process.

- A very special thanks to Virginia Brown and Ron Lewis—fondly known as Mom and Dad.

Nicole Lewis
Brooklyn, NY
April 2013

A Few Notes on Language: It's Not Perfect.

Many of these phrases are simply the best language we have right now to describe what we see. I hope that over time we will be able to develop new language that better holds all the complexity and nuance of our experiences. Until then, here are a few notes on my language usage!

PEOPLE OF COLOR or **POC** refers to people with African, Asian, South Asian, Middle Eastern, Latin, and Native heritage. While we are an extremely diverse and varied group, there are a few major things we have in common. We represent the majority of the people on the globe, and we collectively hold only a very small fraction of the world's wealth and resources. So despite all of our cultural, religious, spiritual, political, and social differences, we are united in the fact that our histories put our communities at the center of this profound inequality.

YOUNG PEOPLE OF COLOR WITH WEALTH. Try to say that five times fast! "Young people of color with wealth" is currently the best language we have for referring to a group of folks who are both of color and have wealth, are building wealth, or come from wealthy or privileged backgrounds. Some may not have inherited money yet, and many never inherit. Although throughout the book I use the term "with wealth," I am also referring to the broader community for whom wealth and money are slightly more complicated.

SOCIAL CHANGE is a phrase that by itself doesn't mean much. The phrase is often used in the world of movement building to refer to the "what" that movement builders are working toward. But without a clear vision of how our society needs to shift, the term "social change" is ineffective. In this book, "social change" refers to change that is progressive, works from the bottom up, and moves both people and institutions toward interdependence and equity.

POWER is the ability to create the world as we see it. It's the ability to set policy, shape our collective history, and advocate for ourselves when we need to. In the United States, the amount of relative power we have is often directly connected to the amount of wealth we hold. A lack of power translates into a lack of access to vital resources, to safety, to the ability to make decisions that can dramatically shift the ways in which we live.

STRUCTURAL RACISM describes the overarching system of racialized discrimination, which is present in the policies and practices of key institutions such as the higher education system, the criminal justice system, financial and lending institutions, health care, or government. Structural racism creates and maintains racialized inequality by privileging whites while discriminating against people of color. The overrepresentation of people of color in prison, the underfunding of public schools in communities of color, and redlining and restrictive covenants are all examples of structural racism.

Here's looking at you.

Although I think people of color without wealth and white people with or without wealth will benefit from checking out the following pages, I had a special group in mind when I sat down to pen these words. I wrote this book for young people of color with wealth.

I am not just writing for and about you.
I am writing straight at you.

I wanted to place you and your lives at the center of this story. I wanted to write so you could hear me. I wanted to write to say, "Hey, I get it because I am you." I wanted to tell our stories so we could see ourselves more fully. I am writing so that we can understand where we fit in—because, although space isn't often made for us, we do belong. I am writing to remind us that we are not alone—there are many of us out there. I am writing so that we begin to see our stories as important and central to working for change.

The stories gathered here reflect all of the people I have met thus far. Without a doubt, there are many more stories waiting to be told about living at the intersection of racism and class privilege. All of our stories are important. So whether we come from a long line of people with inherited wealth, are currently climbing the class ladder, or have class privilege but little money, we need to bring all of our experiences to bear on making social change.

A few notes on what we set out to do here.

This book is an attempt to bring together all the knowledge and lessons learned from organizing people of color with wealth over the past several years. To be sure, the work started well before I entered the picture, but I have been charged with the privilege of sitting down to reflect on how we got here and how far we have come. If everything goes as planned, the wisdom and reflection gathered here will chart the course for the next round of folks of color with wealth who want to take an active role in working for social change. Together we can bring our stories, resources, skills, and knowledge to the proverbial table.

The first iteration of the book profiled the stories of thirteen people of color with wealth who had been involved with Resource Generation and had been working to leverage their resources in the communities they cared about. They were giving money, starting foundations, volunteering time, mentoring young people. All of them were deeply committed to doing what they saw as their part. These thirteen folks knew they could have a huge impact on social change work. In fact, many of them saw their privilege as all the more reason to get involved.

So each committed to talking about their experiences in the hopes that they would be able to open up space for all the other young wealthy people of color to think about their experiences, to think about their vision of a better world, and to figure out what actions they needed to take to make that vision a reality.

When I first started pulling their stories together, I thought about what I wanted to communicate. What needed to be said to wealthy people of color that wasn't being said? What kept us from entering social change work full force? More important, what had these thirteen folks figured out that moved them to action? And what compelled me to organize other rich folks of color? I came up with the following list.

what needed to be said to wealthy people of color that wasn't being said?

I organize because:

I don't want my personal story used to bolster the claim that we now live in a post-racial society. We don't live in a post-racial society and we might not ever, but that is another book. It's not fair to look at the successes of people of color with wealth and make the claim that race is no longer important and that racism is dead.

I don't want my family's successes misconstrued and appropriated as evidence of a "level playing field" or "equal access for all," regardless of skin color, gender, sexuality, ability, or class status. The playing field is not level. With the distribution of wealth increasingly concentrated in the hands of a small few, it's becoming more and more clear that we don't live in a classless, merit-based society. Growing up rich or as any of the many other forms of "right" will help you get ahead and stay ahead.

I believe my successes and upward social and economic movement were made possible by the many people who organized, protested, marched, resisted, created, rebelled, reformed, and agitated for change. My success is a testament to their success, and I want to continue to make change for the generations who will come after me.

More than anything, I have always wanted the freedom to be myself while being Black. The kind of individuality I am working for is something that racism does not allow. I am not striving for the kind of individualism which favors the individual over the collective, but for a life full of expression in which people are valued for their uniqueness while remaining connected to a larger community.

I believe that, in order to achieve these ideals and keep my story, and the stories of people like me, from being used to make false claims about the state of racial progress, wealthy people of color have to bring their experiences and knowledge to bear on social change work. In our experiences lies a key to understanding the complexities and nuances of many forms of privilege and power. We have access to the kinds of stories that highlight the way privilege operates to keep some folks "in" and other folks "out." Even if we have known class privilege all our lives, chances are that just a few generations before us there are stories full of struggle and triumph. Stories which remind us that power is not an abstract concept, but a system of privileges—privileges that extend to a select few based on arbitrary criteria like skin color, gender, or even which college you attended and how much money is in your bank account.

If we can hold all these contradictory stories that make up our personal narratives, then we can examine the way privilege and power are built and maintained and come at a tremendous loss to us all. The first step, of course, is to get our stories out into the open, a task that is much easier said than done. But like the thirteen initial people who provided the inspiration for this project, we have to take stock of our lives in order to participate fully and productively in making social change.

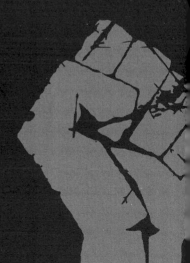

The work starts here and it starts with you.

radical simply means 'grasping things at the root'

ANGELA DAVIS

PART 1

GETTING STARTED

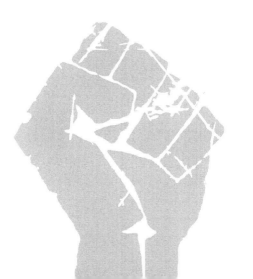

Tracing my steps.

Growing up, I don't remember seeing much of what looked like money. My parents didn't drive fancy cars or show how much they cared through expensive presents. In fact, for quite some time I thought we weren't wealthy. Because I went to a small private high school in Washington, DC, in which the majority of the students came from privileged backgrounds, I thought my classmates were the ones who were wealthy. I did know, however, that I was living differently than many of the Black students I attended school with and many of the Black people I passed while milling around the streets of DC. I knew, too, that my family had a ton of class privilege. My great-grandparents were both Ivy-educated lawyers. They achieved a kind of distinction that is still hard to achieve today at a time when folks of color were openly discriminated against and kept out of many institutions. My family celebrated my great-grandparents' legacy and drew upon their accomplishments as a blueprint for our future successes.

I thought my classmates were the ones who were wealthy

Real life lessons.

The summer after my junior year of college, I worked in DC for the Mayor's Passport to Work Program. Passport to Work provides job readiness training to DC's numerous students who receive free or reduced lunches during the school year. The program's mission is grounded in the fact that, without support from the city in the form of free or reduced lunch, many of these kids would not eat. During the summer, the program provides the students with a little pocket money and gives them a safe place to go while school is out.

Now, I had grown up in and around Washington, DC. But the DC I discovered as part of the Passport to Work Program was a far cry from the DC I knew. What I saw that summer was poverty, public housing, diminished hope, and continued letdowns. The DC I knew, in contrast, was a world of politics, private school, and winter balls, of opportunity and continued praise. I knew that I probably shared space with many of these kids on the subway, and out and about in the city, but we lived worlds apart.

Over the course of the summer, I sailed through a dizzying mix of emotions. Here we were talking about professionalism in the workplace, and meanwhile, in their private and personal lives, these kids were dealing with trauma that could break even the most well-adjusted person. Multiple students had witnessed the death of friends or family. Multiple students had parents or siblings who were addicted to drugs. All of the students knew that they lived in a city that had no idea how bad things really were for them.

Hearing what these kids faced or what they had already experienced in their young lives was difficult, overwhelming, and heartbreaking for me. Adding to my overwhelmed feeling was the fact that most of these kids looked just like me. I wondered, how would my life be different if I were in their shoes? How would theirs be different if they were in mine? What made it possible that we could live in the same small city but live so differently? What made any of this possible, and what would it take to really change their circumstances? Certainly, job readiness training during the summer wasn't going to cut it.

As I got to know my students better and saw just how deep and systemic poverty and racism were, my heartbreak turned into outrage. What I heard over the summer weren't just individual stories about the messed-up things happening in my students' lives. The fact that so many of them had shared experiences wasn't coincidence. What they were illuminating was the shared experience of poverty and racism. The same rules applied to my experience with privilege. The fact that my life looked so different from theirs and that I had more in common with the students with whom I had gone to high school wasn't a coincidence either—it had everything to do with class privilege.

> **if I wanted to see anything change, I would have to play an active role in making that change happen**

I knew enough to understand that my students didn't need me to feel bad for them. No, they had been surviving and living and getting by long before I met them. My personal heartbreak over what they were going through was not going to do anybody any good. Although my heartbreak did help me put my own life and privilege in perspective, my outrage pushed me to get involved. I can say for sure that the shift from heartbreak to outrage facilitated a shift from feeling helpless to a deep understanding of the big picture. My feelings of outrage supported the idea that, if I wanted to see anything change, I would have to play an active role in making that change happen.

Taking it back to the classroom.

When I returned to college after that summer, I joined a dialogue program that sought to help students understand privilege and oppression in their personal lives. I learned about privilege and oppression as forces that affect all of our social identities. Though I had spent all summer looking at poverty, I had put in only minimal work to understand the way privilege showed up in my life. As part of the dialogue program, I learned about the ways in which privilege could make it hard even to see or understand your experiences as privilege. As I learned more about the concept of privilege, I continued to rethink my assumptions about the world around me.

The idea of class privilege blew up my insistence that the most important aspect of wealth was having extra financial resources. I began to think about the significance of coming from a family with generations of advanced degrees, of going to private school, of being part of elite social networks, of owning your own home, of having no debt, of being financially secure, of not having to worry about how to support your next steps, or of having the best health care. I hadn't previously considered how significant these elements had been in my experience of class.

Instead, I began to see how money, though influential in shaping my experiences, was not the only factor that created privilege. I began to wonder if entering private school was about more than just my parents' ability to pay for it. The privilege of having gone to such an elite school was going to help me get into a top college. And graduating from a top college would help me get a high-paying job. And so on and so forth. I could see how my privilege was going to keep building on itself for the rest of my life.

Beginnings.

While participating in a dialogue training one semester, I shared some of my observations about privilege and oppression with another facilitator. We both came from class-privileged backgrounds and had so much in common in terms of the way we saw privilege impacting our lives. We connected over the fact that having a class-privileged background impacted the way we experienced oppression, say, as women, although we also acknowledged that my experiences as a woman of color and her experiences as a white woman were very different. Everywhere we looked, our class privilege mediated the way we experienced our other identities. Intersecting identities wasn't a difficult concept for me to grasp. I thought, again, of my time in DC. My students and I shared a racial identity, but our class backgrounds influenced the way we experienced race, and therefore racism.

During one of our many discussions about class privilege and intersecting identities, my friend shared with me that she was finishing her dissertation on an organization called Resource Generation. Resource Generation's mission, she said, was to organize young people with wealth.

Wait, what?
Organize people with wealth?
I mean, what would we be organizing for?
Isn't organizing a tool for building power in marginalized
  communities?

Questions aside, the idea was intriguing. I was looking for a way to make an impact. But I understood social change work as building power from the bottom up. All of the organizing models I had seen focused on working with people in communities that didn't have access to critical resources. I knew that I wanted to get involved in spite of my privilege, but up until that day it had seemed like the only option I had was to participate in work led by people of color without acknowledging my class background. Was it possible that something meaningful could come out of organizing around my own story, of organizing around intersecting identities and privilege?

STEPHANIE'S BIG QUESTIONS

" *When I left school, I got connected with some local non-profits, and as I continued to do work around women's issues and human rights issues, I realized how much of the work was single-issue. I don't see the world as single issues. I don't have just one single identity. There's so much difference and possibility and complexity. I don't really think we can change people's lives if we're only focusing on whether or not they have food on the table. There are so many other factors! I started to think about where I could be to have a meta-view.*

That is when I started looking at philanthropy. The philanthropic organizations I came into contact with in the Bay Area were looking at much larger issues. The Women's Foundation is a very political public foundation that instituted a community grant-making process in order to have community input. Working in the foundation world raised all kinds of questions. I was grappling with my values and my vision of social justice, and I wondered, "What does that look like in philanthropy? How do you include philanthropy as a partner in social justice?"

Nevertheless, I signed on to help my newfound friend and doctoral candidate finish her research. As part of the deal, I got to attend Resource Generation's annual conference Making Money Make Change (MMMC) to witness the work firsthand. In the weeks leading up to MMMC, despite all the work I had done so far, I had a number of freak-outs and revelations about the privilege in my life. I thought:

I don't have a trust fund.
I am not really rich.
My only claim to wealth and privilege is through my family.
It's not like mine *mine.*
I don't know the first thing about philanthropy.
I haven't written a zine or any cool books about the work
   I am doing.
Am I down enough?   Am I rich enough? Am I cool enough?

But by the opening circle, I was actually feeling pretty good. Here was a group of people asking the same questions that I was. Questions that focused on what was going on in the world and what we could do about it as people with class privilege.

By the end of MMMC, I started thinking that maybe organizing people with privilege was possible. After all, we had financial resources, and, even if we didn't, we had connections to powerful people. If we could figure out a way to put those resources to good use, maybe we could have a real impact. Could the power that comes with class privilege be leveraged to support social change movements?

When the opportunity came up to join the Resource Generation team to organize young people of color with wealth, I jumped at the chance.

Over the years: Are we even rich?

Over the past several years with Resource Generation, I have met a number of amazing young people with wealth who are all looking for a way to make a difference.

Some came to RG from the world of philanthropy because they were looking to maximize the effectiveness of their giving. Some just wanted to "give back." Others came to RG from academia, where they had been thinking, writing, and philosophizing about the intersection of race and class in the history of organizing for change. Still others came to us from organizing with other people of color to push for major changes in our political and economic system. Even though we were entering into this work from vastly different places, the one thing that united us was that we all cared about making real and lasting change.

Despite the fact that we all believed in the need for this kind of change, we had a number of questions about our work. Some of us wondered whether or not we could really make change as a community of people with wealth. Or if we even truly belonged in a group of wealthy folks. Others wondered if working in communities of privilege facilitated anything other than a consolidation of privilege. Some contemplated whether their wealth was actually a reflection of racial progress. Certainly, all of us wondered what it would take for racism to be finally uprooted in our society.

some of us wondered whether or not we could really make change as a community of people with wealth

Then, there was one question that stopped many of us right in our tracks: Are we even rich? Time and again we would puzzle together about what it meant to be rich or have wealth. We questioned if people of color could actually be rich, given the grand scheme of global wealth. We wondered if there was some qualifying level we had to reach before considering ourselves rich. Did a high income make us wealthy? Did we have to have assets too? Did we need to have intergenerational wealth to be truly rich? We wondered where we fell on the wealth distribution spectrum. Top ten percent or five percent? How did we measure up to other wealthy people in our community?

WHAT IS WEALTH? JAMES AND RICK WEIGH IN

JAMES: *Most people consider wealth to be enough financial stability where you don't need to work; you work because you want to. But with my educational background alone and what I look forward to doing in my life throughout my career, I feel that I'm already wealthy. I don't live paycheck to paycheck or anything like that, and I do see the defined potential of wealth in my future or near future.*

RICK: *People define wealth in different ways. I believe that there's a difference between money and wealth. One is tangible, which is inheriting property and status. Whereas money is simply what you earn. Wealth gives a certain level of security.*

Here we go! What do wealth and class privilege really look like?

The one thing I know for sure is that no one is immune to having some seriously conflicted, messed-up, often hilarious, and difficult thoughts and feelings about money, race, and making change. All of this can make it hard to answer the most fundamental question of whether or not we even have wealth or class privilege. Some of the signs aren't as obvious as you'd think. So I put together a little list.

Chances are if several of these experiences apply to you, you're probably like me—a young person with wealth.

1. *You have a lot of money (it's the simplest way to tell).*

2. *You have no debt.*

3. *While growing up you went to sleepaway camp, traveled, or did not have to work during the summer.*

4. *Your passion for the visual and performing arts was encouraged—with no expectation that you would turn your talent into a lucrative career.*

5. *You aren't sure what it is your parents do, but you know they are well paid.*

6. *You face tremendous pressure from your parents (or Tiger Mom) to continue your family's legacy of success. Bonus points if you can top it.*

7. *You were cared for consistently by a paid employee who was not a member of your family.*

8. *After college, while your friends were worrying about getting a job to pay off student loans, you traveled.*

9. *You changed your major three times as you continued to discover your life's purpose, and it took you six years to graduate—all without debt. And you have a secret masters degree in Finnish Studies.*

10. *You or your parents/grandparents own their own profitable business.*

11. *You are able to travel frequently to the country where your parents or grandparents were born and/or you have dual citizenship.*

12. *You or your family members have a financial advisor, you are a financial advisor, or you are your family's financial advisor.*

13. *You suspect your parents are rich, but when you asked, they neither confirmed nor denied your suspicion, and you left the conversation even more confused.*

14. *You belong to a social network in which most people would probably answer yes to one or more of the items on this list. Or, you dropped out of a social network because most of the people in it would probably answer yes to one or more of the items on this list.*

15. *You have never made a budget and you aren't sure what your living expenses are, but you've always had enough money to cover what you needed and then some.*

16. *You are a legacy at an Ivy League University or other Tier One University.*

17. *You can afford to choose where you live, whether it's in a trendy urban neighborhood or somewhere less expensive.*

18. *You and/or your family members have assets: houses, cars, savings, investments. And if you need a deposit or down*

*payment to support your next steps, your family can help
you out.*

19. *When you need professional help, such as a top lawyer or
broker, your family can connect you to their personal network of
peers in the field.*

20. *You can afford to work an unpaid summer internship or
prestigious fellowship to build your résumé.*

This list probably isn't what comes up when most people think
about wealth. Certainly having money and material things is an
aspect of class privilege, but it is not necessarily a prerequisite.
It is possible to have tremendous amounts of class privilege and
very little financial wealth. Access to key institutions, powerful
networks, and vacations and the ability to choose where we live
are all very tangible benefits of class privilege. Class privilege is
about more than money— it is about our experiences.

For example,

SAY YOU WANTED TO PURSUE A CAREER IN PUBLIC RELATIONS...
Maybe your parents made "the call" to their friends in the indus-
try. Voilà, you've got a job.

SAY YOU WANTED TO TAKE SOME TIME OFF AFTER GRADUATION...
Maybe you needed to figure out your life's purpose. Maybe you
wanted to see the world. Who knows? Well, without the safety net
of class privilege plus economic security, taking time off to find
anything other than a job would be a risky move, but you were
able to make it work.

SAY YOU WANTED TO BUY A HOUSE...

Maybe you didn't have the money, but when you shared your plans with your family, they jumped at the chance to help you out. So, they co-signed on a loan, provided you with seed money, or connected you to their lawyer friends and other professionals to help you embark on the next stage of your life.

THIS IS CLASS PRIVILEGE AT WORK. Class privilege is about what social networks we belong to and how easily we can call upon the people in those networks to provide us with their skills and expertise, a job, advice, or a career-making introduction. While most young people are considering their next steps based on how soon they have to start paying back student loans after graduation or based on the need to earn money to secure their future, we have

DEV'S STORY

" *I grew up in a small town of 300,000 on the west coast of British Columbia, called Victoria BC. I was raised in an even smaller neighborhood that had its own fire department, private schools, soccer team, and three-person police force. It was fairly idyllic. I was one of a handful of other East Indian kids that attended my high school— one of them being my brother.*

My story is about what I learned. I learned how to act, how to be, what to talk about, and what it meant to go to someone's cabin, or play rugby. I learned how to have a conversation that was engaging, funny, relevant, and drew on examples that people understood and would know how to laugh at.

What I learned was a hidden curriculum of class privilege that I didn't realize I actually had been through, and aced.

been able to make decisions based mainly on what we want to do. Even if we don't have direct access to cash, the privileges that come with our status have set us up to live well. Fundamentally, class privilege is about social positioning and proximity to power.

A Complicated Intersection.

As people of color, our experiences with class privilege are complicated by our experiences with racism. If class privilege is about access to power in the form of resources and institutions, then racism is a denial of access to these same resources and institutions. In contrast to class privilege, which makes it easier to live well, racism makes it hard for people of color to individually and collectively get ahead. People of color with wealth, then, simultaneously have access to power through class privilege and are denied power on account of their race. No matter how much money we have or how wide and deep our privileged network is, racism is a part of our experience too.

Class Privilege + Racism.

Class privilege can serve as a shield against the most marginalizing aspects of racism. Our access to resources means we have greater social and economic mobility—a strange contradiction to the logic of structural racism. Access to resources means we can afford private education and avoid schools that are not set up to support their students. Access to resources means we can choose where we live—in neighborhoods that are safe and close to the goods and services we use daily. Access to resources means we are less likely to come into contact with police violence, to be victims of predatory lending, or to receive inadequate or no health care at all.

On the other hand, although class privilege alters our experience of racism, it does not altogether eliminate it from our lives. For example, class privilege won't keep us from being targeted by the police, but it will dramatically affect the outcome of our interaction. If we find ourselves on the wrong side of the law, we can draw upon our resources to help us navigate the criminal justice system. We have the money to cover any fines or fees incurred. We have the money and connections to find a good lawyer. Without the benefit of financial resources, our experience navigating the criminal justice system would be dramatically different. For many poor and working class people of color, court fees and fines pose a major financial burden and a lack of adequate representation or no representation at all makes for an unfair trial.

Another important example of class privilege's buffering effect on racism is our access to the tools and resources needed to heal from traumatic experiences. We can quit stressful jobs with bigoted bosses. We can go to therapy to work out painful memories or experiences around race and other elements of our lives. We can take vacations when we need to recharge, or attend to our bodies with massage or acupuncture to aid us in getting through our daily struggles. To be sure, healing is an essential part of resisting racism. Racism takes a toll on our bodies, minds, and spirits. In this light, healing is a form of resistance. To be able to take the time to care for ourselves when we experience trauma—whether it's racialized or not—is a huge, and often unrecognized, benefit of class privilege.

we don't always directly experience some of the worst aspects of racial inequality

Living at the intersection of class privilege and racism means that we don't always directly experience some of the worst aspects of racial inequality. Still, racism does show up for people of color with wealth in a number of ways—often in the form of interpersonal racism. Of course, our experiences can also be very different depending on the communities of color we are from and the shade of our skin. But racism is present when we are expected to "represent" our race because we are one of the handful of people of color in our neighborhoods, schools, or places of work. It's present when we are questioned about the authenticity of our racial identity. Racism is present when we are silenced or overlooked by our peers in school or in our workplace. Racism is present when someone tells a racially insensitive joke in our presence, but suggests that it's "not about you, because, well, you're different."

Wrapping our minds around the intersection of racism and class privilege can be daunting. For starters, our individual experiences are often at odds with the experiences of people of color who are not wealthy. In fact, our experience of racism may look so different that it may feel unfair to name it "racism." Across most communities of color, the number of people who hold wealth is tiny in comparison to the number who are poor, middle, or working class. The difficulty we may have in naming racism in our lives is a reflection of how structural racism has stifled people of color's overall economic gains. The more we look at race and racism in our lives, the more we will uncover the many, many ways in which race and class are deeply intertwined.

> **our experience of racism may look so different that it may feel unfair to name it "racism"**

The BIG Picture.

There is nothing fair or correct or good or justified about racism. There is nothing fair about the fact that our class background means we don't have to face racism's worst, hardest, and most life-threatening aspects. It is easy to be weighed down by the idea that racism is present in the lives of all people of color. Certainly, this is not a novel idea, but taking the time to sit with the notion opens the door to all of the thoughts and all of the feelings we may find difficult to face. For me, looking at racism head-on brings up a number of questions. Time and again I just keep coming back to one: What the fuck?

we are connected by our shared experience of racism

The only thing that helps to dissolve the weight I feel when thinking about racism is the fact that, throughout history, communities of color have pushed back against racism to improve not only their lives, but the lives of all people of color present and future. Although we may be part of our wealthy communities and although we may, at times, feel disconnected from the larger community of people of color, we are connected by our shared experience of racism. Which means we have a stake in the current movement of people pushing for racial and economic justice. We have a stake in creating real change in our lives and in the lives of all people of color. No matter how we are positioned, racism is part of our lives, part of the lives of the people we care about, and part of the institutions we participate in.

The struggle is indeed our struggle too.

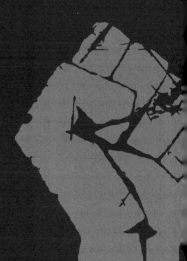

Storytellers are a threat.

They threaten all champions of control, they frighten usurpers of the right-to-freedom of the human spirit—in state, in church or mosque, in party congress, in the university or wherever.

CHINUA ACHEBE

PART 2

RADICAL VOICES

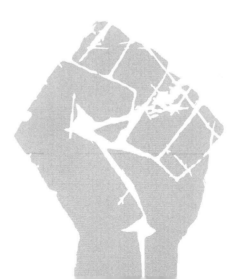

First Drafts.

In the beginning, my money story looked something like this:

I come into wealth and class privilege from both sides of my family. On my mom's side, my great-grandparents were both Ivy-educated lawyers. They ran a private practice in Philadelphia and were very influential in working to desegregate the city. My mom grew up with the benefits of her family's status. My dad grew up working class in Virginia. He received a full scholarship to go to college, studied engineering, and received another scholarship to go to graduate school. He has built wealth working in the field of information technology over the course of my lifetime.

I was afraid that digging into the past or asking specific questions about money could stir up drama

Pretty straightforward, right? This is the story I was told, and it's the story I stuck with for a long time. I was afraid that digging into the past or asking specific questions about money could stir up drama. What if I appeared money hungry in the eyes of my family? Plus, I couldn't imagine asking my dad probing questions about his financial success. After all, if he wanted to tell me the details, he'd had many years to do so. Sure, I could think about my own experiences with class privilege, but when it came to getting my family to open up, it felt a little too personal.

As I started to talk to more people about their own money stories, I noticed that my fear and hesitation about asking questions was not uncommon. Whether people had inherited wealth or were building it in their lifetimes, most of us didn't talk openly about our experiences. Our families operated on a need-to-know basis, which meant that if we didn't need to know the details about how the wealth was made, we didn't know them. And those who were building wealth tended to shy away from talking specifics too. So instead we all just relied on the stories we were told—stories that gave us the illusion that our families were proper and pulled together, and that building wealth as people of color was without complication. Our stories made it look like there was never any pain, confusion, guilt, or trauma mixed up with money.

The personal is political.

I decided that it was time to start asking some questions. I quickly realized that I had a ton of them....

How much money are we talking about?
Is it rapidly cloning itself in the stock market?
Invested in gold?
Tied up in war bonds?
Or just stuffed into a mattress?
WHERE IS THE MONEY?
And who makes the decisions about it?

I wanted to ask my dad what motivated him to make money. Did he love his job? What did he have to give up to make money? Did he have any regrets? Did he face racism and glass ceilings in the workplace? What problems had having money solved? Or did "more money more problems" ring true?

I wanted to ask my mom if the privilege she had inherited had changed the way she lived. Did class privilege impact the way she related to other people of color? What was it like to come of age during the civil rights movement? What did it mean to have class privilege as a person of color at this time? How did she benefit from it? Did she feel connected to the struggle? Did she wish that she could hide her privilege? Or was she proud of her class background?

what was it like to go to all-white schools?

I wanted to go back in time and ask my great-grandparents what it was like to take on racism in their work. And what was it like to go to all-white schools? How did they cope with discrimination and intolerance from their peers? How did they define success—as money and accomplishment or as what they were able to achieve for the common good? Were there times when they hoped class privilege would protect them, but it didn't? How did they make sense of their success in the face of racial inequality and discrimination?

With all these questions bubbling in my mind, I started to get a clearer picture of what was missing from my money story. There was no mention of struggle, difficult choices, messiness, confusion, uncertainty. Of the losses we had faced in order to make the gains. And there was no mention of history, governmental policies, or social justice movements. But it seemed unlikely to me that my family members, especially when they were living during such distinct periods of social transformation, hadn't faced any turmoil while going after their dreams.

After weeks of sitting with my money story and wondering why the version I'd been taught was missing all the hard parts, I had a major *aha!* moment. I realized that my family story echoed another story I'd been hearing my whole life. The story of the classic American Dream: Even if you have nothing, you can pull yourself up by the bootstraps, work hard, get educated. And if you're smart enough and work hard enough, you will succeed. In the myth of the American Dream, everyone has a fair shot at becoming wealthy, and everyone who succeeds does so by their own merit.

ANASTASIA'S AMERICAN DREAM

" *My dad immigrated to the United States for college and ended up earning several degrees in engineering that assured him employment at numerous government agencies and private businesses. He became very prosperous from these jobs and became even wealthier after he invested his money into ventures, stocks, and properties.*

However, his story also represents the limited power of money.

Family money paid for his education at the University of California, Berkeley, but institutionalized racism kept him out of the East Coast Ivy League schools that he desperately wanted to attend. His background and education did not guarantee that he would receive well-deserved promotions at work in the 1940s. Success as a businessman did not protect him from his suburban neighbors' violent threats when he organized migrant workers in my hometown during the 1970s and 1980s.

The stories of people of color with wealth map so well onto this template. We didn't just go from rags to riches—we overcame discrimination and proved our merit by rising up to make the most of our lives. And in some ways, that is true. I don't want to minimize my family's hard work. I am proud of everything they have accomplished. Sometimes I find myself in awe of my great-grandparents. It's exciting to think about how they defied the odds and overcame all the barriers that racism created. I find strength and a sense of pride in being able to tell their story in a way that makes it appear exceptional.

I don't want to minimize my family's hard work

SHREYA'S PRIVILEGE

" I counter variations of "You went to Columbia University?!? You are so smart!" with an explanation: "Well, a big reason I could go to Columbia is because of my class privilege." It feels really important to talk about my privilege to counter the various ways that classism plays into concepts of meritocracy. There were so many opportunities I had (and still have) access to in my development that I know other people of color don't have.

Growing up I was able to participate in travel-study and no- or low-paying prestigious programs. I had time and money to dedicate to reading and developing my art hobby into a real possibility and potential paying gig rather than working in a position I didn't feel moved my goals forward. Even social resources such as advice and guidance over the last 20 years on applications, career choices, and program and school options were available to me because of my privilege.

However, that very exceptionalism is also the problem with my money story—and with the story of the American Dream. When I tell my money story in a way that makes my parents and great-grandparents look exceptional, I am also implying that individual merit is all it takes to succeed, and that anyone who hasn't been able to transcend racism to accumulate wealth just wasn't smart enough or didn't work hard enough.

exceptionalism is also the problem with my money story— and with the story of the American Dream

I certainly did not mean to be telling that kind of story! I don't think we all have equal access to quality education. I certainly don't think we live in a meritocracy in which everything we have is a reflection of how hard we work. I think structural racism, sexism, and classism create all kinds of inequality. I think policy plays a huge role in determining who gets ahead and who falls behind. I know all this from my own experiences with class privilege.

The truth is that my family's story wouldn't even have been possible without the power of collective action and the movements that fought against racism. In fact, my great-grandparents achieved success as lawyers by being a part of those movements and taking on racial discrimination in the city of Phila-

my family's story wouldn't even have been possible without the power of collective action

delphia. And my parents were part of the first generation of Black students to attend integrated schools. Their access to "equal education" was made possible by the gains of the civil rights movement. And I know that all of the shifts and changes I want for our future are going to require collective action too. I don't want to lose the part of my story that supports the importance of social change organizing.

How to Write a New Money Story

A money story is the tale of how your wealth or the wealth in your family was made. Whether that story has been passed down through generations or you are the first person to tell it, odds are your money story as it stands right now is missing some crucial details.

IF YOU'RE READY TO START REWRITING, HERE ARE SOME QUESTIONS THAT CAN HELP:

Does your story focus mainly on one person creating wealth solely through hard work, smarts, and sacrifice?

What other factors may have played a role?

How does your story compare with that of others in your community?

How have institutions created access and/or blocked access to resources?

How are histories of oppression a part of your story?

What role do experiences of racism play in your money story?

How might they intersect with other experiences of both privilege and oppression?

Are there pieces of the story about pain, loss, survival, and resilience that are missing?

What happens when you place your story in a larger context and look at it within histories of racism, colonialism, and movements of resistance?

SOME POSSIBLE FACTORS TO THINK ABOUT:

Family	Community	Culture	Race
Ethnicity	Skin Color/ Shade	Ability and Access	Gender
Sexuality	Marriage	Religion	Spiritual Practice
Privilege	Immigration Status	Protest and Protest Movements	Status in Country of Origin
Internment Camps	Genocide	Colonialism	Slavery
Violence	War	Land Ownership	Education
Connections	Relationships with Banks and Investors	Policies Like Redlining	US Wealth-Building Programs Like the GI Bill
Tax Breaks	Subsidies and Grants	Government Connections and Contracts	Labor Trafficking
Isolation	Inheritance or Loss	Resistance	Survival

The last thing I want my money story to do is to suggest that since my family was able to accumulate wealth despite the obstacles of racism, there's no need for structural racism to change. Or that racism is eliminated when people of color build wealth and gain access to power. Just because a small group of people of color can accumulate wealth doesn't mean that the entire economic system isn't still rigged against people of color in general. Economic disempowerment can't change until structural racism changes in every institution, from criminal justice to banks to real estate. I don't want my story or the stories of other young people of color with wealth to be used to justify an unfair economic system. But until we start telling the parts of our stories we've been taught to leave out—the parts about struggle, community and collective action, the intersections of class and race—we're in danger of doing just that.

As bell hooks writes in *Class Matters*:

"Radical [...] voices, especially those with some degree of class privilege, must have the courage to talk about class. Racial solidarity in anti-racist struggle can, sometimes does, and must coexist with a recognition of the importance of ending class elitism."

Do we have the courage to be those radical voices who talk about class?

And if yes, how do we do it?

Human progress is neither automatic nor inevitable.

Even a superficial look at history reveals that no social advance rolls in on the wheels of inevitability. Every step towards the goal of justice requires sacrifice, suffering, and struggle; the tireless exertions and passionate concern of dedicated individuals.

MARTIN LUTHER KING, JR.

PART 3

WHERE THE WORK BEGINS

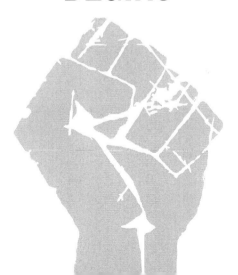

First steps toward action.

In early spring of 2012, RG launched our first praxis group for people of color. Here we were: six relative strangers who saw a flier for a group for people of color with wealth and thought,

Yes, finally, a space for me.

OK, maybe we didn't say it out loud, but certainly some part of us must have felt a sense that this space would be different from all the other social change spaces we had been part of (or avoided)—because this space was explicitly by and for us. In the weeks leading up to our first meeting, I imagined what our time together would be like: productive brainstorming sessions, moving conversations about how we had been affected by racism or how our lives had benefited from privilege, and lists of actions we could take together.

we shared our frustrations about being invisible or misunderstood

The first day of our meeting I got everything I wanted and more. We started off with nervous laughter as we spent time getting to know each other. We talked about what wealth looked like in our lives and how we made sense of the contradicting messages we received as people of color with wealth. We shared our frustrations about being invisible or misunderstood on account of our backgrounds.

As the months rolled on, we turned our attention to the organizing and movement building going on around us. Everyone had an opinion about the merits of the current Occupy movement, or about the effects of new immigration policy, or whether or not the new health care legislation would hold up in court. We spent hours comparing and contrasting the effects of poverty in American inner cities versus the poverty many of us had witnessed firsthand while travelling or visiting family in the Global South. We pondered: Was the presence of the police in the inner city stifling much-needed underground economies? How does structural racism compound the effects of poverty in the US? How much deeper could we go? I wondered.

Somewhere in the middle of a heated conversation about poverty, though, I realized we had already spent months talking and theorizing about the world around us. We were friends now—we'd traded our nervous laughter for open communication. But we had yet to ask ourselves what role we wanted to play in addressing the disparities we spoke so passionately about. After all, it was a praxis group—we were here to put theory into action, so at some point we would have to address the question of action. Besides, wasn't taking action really what we were here for? Was talking about issues easier for all of us than taking action? Even though the conversation was compelling, I decided right then and there to throw out the question that was rattling around in my head. "So, what are we going to do about it? I mean, what is our role in it all?" I pushed further. "If we've got resources...what do we do with them?" For a long minute all we could do was stare at each other in silence. If we've got resources, what are we going to do with them?

if we've got resources... what do we do with them?

How to get started.

It turns out that the first step toward taking action isn't as complicated as you might think. In fact, we had already taken action by coming together in our praxis group—and you're already on your way just by picking up this book. Thinking through our experiences with wealth, class, and racial or ethnic identity is what makes planning our next steps possible. And by doing it together, we can support each other to tackle the most challenging questions and stick to the plans that we make.

we can support each other to tackle the most challenging questions and stick to the plans that we make

Some people like to start out by doing some writing or reading on their own. Others jump in with a conversation. You may already have a friend or family member in mind to talk with—maybe they even share some similar experiences with you. If you're not used to talking about your access to resources or if money is a taboo subject in your family, it might be a little harder to get a first conversation started. In that case, an easy answer is to get in touch with Resource Generation and come to a dinner or a conference or join a praxis group. That's why RG is here!

First Steps: Asking Questions

You may already have a bunch of questions you want to start with. But here are a few more you can use as writing prompts whether you're alone, with a friend, or in a group.

How has my class privilege or access to wealth and other material resources been useful to me?

Are there ways it has provided me protection and opportunities?

Are there ways it has divided me from other people in my family? From other communities of color? From poor and working class people?

What is my vision of social change? What inspires me? How has my racial or ethnic identity influenced my vision? How have my experiences with wealth or class privilege influenced my vision?

And if you'd like to keep reading—or maybe even share an article with a friend or start a book group together—here are some options to start with:

CLASSIFIED: HOW TO STOP HIDING YOUR PRIVILEGE AND USE IT FOR SOCIAL CHANGE
by Karen Pittelman & Resource Generation

THE COLOR OF WEALTH: THE STORY BEHIND THE U.S. RACIAL WEALTH DIVIDE
by Meizhu Lui, Barbara Robles, Betsy Leondar-Wright, Rose Brewer, and Rebecca Adamson, with United for a Fair Economy

RESOURCE GENERATION'S BLOG: *www.resourcegeneration.org/blog*

As we move through this work, we are going to need a team of folks around us for moral support. It makes a big difference to have people around who share your experience when you're trying to unpack the complicated intersections of race and class privilege. It helps to know other people are having similar freakouts or hitting parallel roadblocks, and that you aren't the only one making your way through all of these tough questions.

we might not notice that sometimes we just assume we know best or should be in charge no matter what

We can also look to other young people of color with wealth to challenge us when we're falling back on class patterns. Especially if we grew up with class privilege, there may be ways we've been taught to be in the world that don't always match up with our social change values. For example, we might not notice that sometimes we just assume we know best or should be in charge no matter what. Or we might have trouble committing to things because we've always had so many options open to us.

One class privilege pattern that can definitely get in the way of taking action is perfectionism. If we feel like we always have to be perfect, it's easy to get so afraid of mistakes that we freeze and never make any decisions at all. We can help remind each other that we don't need to have all the answers or be "the authority" to get involved. In fact, entering social change work with more questions than answers has its advantages. It means we get to listen to other voices and practice following the lead of people who are most affected by the unjust systems we want to change. We get to learn from the experiences of those who have been working in social change for years.

As we try on new ways of being in community and taking action, we are going to make lots of gaffes along the way. But with the support and challenge of our peers, we can remind each other that it's OK to mess up, process our mistakes, and keep moving.

Sharing Resources.

Sharing resources is a crucial part of taking action as young people with wealth. One way to do it is by donating to social change movements. All too often, grassroots groups that are struggling for real change are not supported by mainstream philanthropy and have a hard time raising money. Giving to this kind of work means we have the chance to support communities who have been most affected by injustice while they work to transform the world in which we live. Plus, we can leverage our giving by using our access and connections to spread the word to other donors.

we can leverage our giving by using our access and connections to spread the word to other donors

Helping our communities build financial assets is another important form that sharing resources can take. This may mean supporting family members here or abroad, or investing in local businesses, homes, and loan funds. To zoom out for a minute: Structural racism has disadvantaged people of color socially and economically on a global scale for a long time. As folks of color with wealth, even though we personally may be giving money away, we have a major role to play in supporting communities of color to develop assets that support our self-determination while maintaining interdependence.

Of course, figuring out what that role looks like isn't simple. There are some big questions here. For example: What does it mean to be in solidarity with each other as people of color from various class backgrounds and different communities of color? Does wealth accumulation always lead to greater power and economic security in communities of color? Is a more just distribution of wealth the responsibility of individuals or the government—or both?

These kinds of questions can be just the tip of the iceberg when it comes to deciding how much of our resources we should use, invest, save, or give. It can be especially hard to answer how much is enough to save when we think about

we know what a difference having resources has made in our lives

what it means to live as people of color in a world marked by racism. We know what a difference having resources has made in our lives. But even savings can be put to work for social change. We can divest from companies we don't believe in or vote our shares to help change their policies. And we can channel our money into socially responsible investing, community-run projects, and loan funds.

ANASTASIA ON GIVING

" *To my father, money is a tool to do good in the world. That is his whole mission in life: He wants to do good in the world. So much of my dad's culture is very community-oriented and philanthropic in nature. At the same time, my father has something very unique to any culture. He's a mixture of so many different worlds. I think all of his different experiences have made him so open. When he was creating the wealth, his dream was always to be able to do something for the world with it.*

One first step toward sharing resources is to gather our personal financial information. After all, it's hard to determine how much to give or save if you don't know what you have! And if you don't know all the answers (or even any of the answers), don't worry—you're not the only one. This is a tricky step for many of us, especially if you are an inheritor and weren't the one who made many of the financial decisions that now affect you. Ironing out all the details may take some time. But that doesn't mean you have to wait to take action! With just a little research and planning, you can get started now.

NITIKA'S JOURNEY

For a long time, I didn't even question or realize my class privilege. Once I started to get politicized, I went through the usual phases of shock, guilt, pain, and secrecy about my process. But over time, it was through communicating openly about it with other people (from various class backgrounds), and through being called out about it many times, that I was able to grow and move.

I believe wealth and class privilege allow me to know that I have choices, and give me the freedom to make choices independently, sometimes even in isolation.

But, what I am now increasingly aware of and working on is a struggle for connection and togetherness. My hope is that one day we will collectively work through these questions: "How much is enough for us?" "How best can we include a cross-class community in making decisions about redistribution of our excess wealth?"

First Steps: Thinking about Giving, Saving, Spending, and Investing

There are lots more worksheets in RG's book *Classified* that can help you research your financial information and come up with a detailed action plan. In the meantime, here are some ideas for possible first steps.

1. *What do you know about the resources you have access to? What about resources you may have access to in the future, like trusts or investments? If there are other people who have control over your finances, do you know who they are? What is one step you can take to find out more?*

2. *Do you have a budget or a clear sense of your expenses? If not, try an experiment: first, estimate your monthly expenses. Then make a commitment to tracking your expenses for a month. How close were you to your estimate? Understanding your expenses better is a key part of any financial planning.*

3. *What is one thing you would like to learn about socially responsible investing? Take 30 minutes to research it and learn more. (Check out the Resource Library on RG's website under Financial Planning: www.resourcegeneration.org/resources/resource-library/financial-planning)*

4. *How many people are supported by your own or your family's assets right now? What kind of family financial responsibilities might you hold in the future? Schedule a time to talk about this with someone (a family member? your partner? a financial advisor?) who can help you find out more.*

5. *Take 20 minutes to do some writing and visioning about the future. Here's a writing prompt to use: How much money would be enough to support a healthy, sustainable life for you? For your family? Your community? The world? What role do other factors besides money play in creating that life?*

6. *Do you have a giving plan or a way of determining how much you give and where? If not, have you ever given money away before?*

If you've given money before, try making a list of some of the causes and communities you have supported in the past. Do you see any common themes? What kind of decision-making process did you use? How do you feel about the decisions you've made so far?

If you've never given any money away before, take a quick look at your bank account. Could you afford to give $100 right now? What about more? There's bound to be at least one social change organization whose work you're excited about. Why not send them a check right now? Getting started is that simple!

7. *What are some traditions of giving in your family or community? Are there parts of these traditions you want to make a part of the way that you share your resources? What is one way you could do this?*

Bringing our whole selves.

When it comes to taking action for social change, we have a lot we can bring to the table—not just resources. We can bring our skills, our time, and our passion. We can bring our whole selves to the work.

JOAQUIN GETS INVOLVED

" For so long, I felt as though I wasn't in a certain income level so I couldn't be philanthropic. Young people need to understand that they can start giving very early. They might not be able to give financially, but they can give time, energy, and input, and all these things are valuable to organizations and causes.

Part of what can feel scary about taking action like this is that it often means having to talk about our class backgrounds with other people. What if it's awkward? What if everyone dislikes us? Especially as people of color, we might not want to risk doing anything to disrupt our connection to a community we rely on.

But being open also means that we can strategize with others about how to tap our connections. We can talk about strategy, about what an organization or a movement or a community member might really need and how we can help. It also allows us to build relationships that are grounded in honesty instead of always worrying that our secret might get out and change the way people see us. Most important, talking openly about our experiences with privilege both to people who share our race and class backgrounds and to those across race and class lines gives us the chance to build a collective understanding of the ways that class and race intersect, and to take action from that place.

We can also commit ourselves to being in community with people of color from all backgrounds who are working for social change, to being a part of something much bigger than ourselves. All too often, folks of color are isolated within their own racial and ethnic communities. When we separate into groups, we lose out on making connections within the broad, global community of people of color. Our smaller cultural networks are incredibly important and provide numerous forms of support. But being separated along ethnic or religious lines can make it difficult to remember the fact that we are actually a global majority. Claiming the broad community of people of color while acknowledging that we have vastly different experiences with racism, class privilege, and other systems of oppression is politically powerful.

STEPHANIE'S *AHA!* MOMENT

I do social justice work with institutions, as a philanthropic advisor to social justice organizations, and in my work as an artist and filmmaker. My work within institutions has decreased over time. I became irritated when I would have great conversations with individual members of a foundation, but the culture of the institution itself would not shift overall. I had an aha! moment in which I realized my biggest impact was at the individual level. I can have a bigger impact with how I build and sustain relationships. For example, I am part of the Ruckus Society, a grassroots organization led by people of color, and I am on the host committee for an event they are organizing. I can bring in my contacts and help the Ruckus Society build relationships with people who are interested in helping. This way I am directly supporting their work.

Taking leadership?

If we're bringing our whole selves to the task of taking action, then does that mean we also should be stepping into leadership roles? Yes! There's definitely a need for more youth of color leadership in social change work. Developing our skills and being visible in that work as young people of color is important. As people with wealth, though, it can also be complicated.

On the one hand, it's worth considering class patterns. If we've been taught to always take charge or that we always know what's best, we might have a tendency to rush into leadership a little too quickly. It's worth taking a step back and asking if maybe this is a moment where everyone might benefit from someone else—especially someone who has the experience of being raised poor or working class—taking the lead. It might make sense for us to lead sometimes, but asking the question is an important part of bringing a class analysis to everything we do.

Taking on leadership can also feel complicated because the intersection of class privilege and racism can sometimes lead us to feel tokenized. Some organizations are hungry for the leadership of young people of color only because it can superficially boost their reputation as progressive and diverse. In situations like this, our class privilege can make us look like the perfect candidates for a job. On top of being young and people of color, we are well-spoken, have fancy degrees, and come with important connections that can help with fundraising. At times, it can be hard to tell whether or not we're being offered a genuine leadership opportunity where the group will value our input.

On the other hand, social change work needs all the leaders it can get. That means us! As young people of color with wealth in community, we can challenge each other both to step forward and to step back. We can talk together about our decisions and what it feels like to take on more responsibility. We also are in the perfect position to be leaders by organizing where we come from and helping other young people with wealth take action. Getting started is simple—can you think of another young person with wealth you know who believes in social change but isn't connected to any of this work? Maybe it's time to reach out.

SHREYA WEIGHS IN

" *I've hidden a lot of parts of myself over the years, mostly because I needed to deal with my own story before I could share it with others.*

In college, while everyone else seemed to be creating lifelong friendships, I never let myself get close enough to anyone to talk about the history of abuse and depression that I was constantly dealing with. I never felt fully known. There was something always partly hidden. Most of the time I wasn't ready to open up about what I was struggling with—in doing so, I would have had to be more open about my background and the associated social and financial resources that come with it.

But because not speaking up is such a large point of separation from communities and people I care a lot about, I find it important to speak up more and more. I appreciate the way my friends take care of my story. Their care has helped me understand my own story better.

A few encouraging words.

Over my years working at Resource Generation, I have seen young people of color with wealth put their privilege to work for change in so many amazing ways. We are leveraging our connections and sharing our resources. We are helping to fund grassroots organizing. We are volunteering time to community-based organizations, advocating for paying our fair share of taxes, and divesting from corporations who seek profit at the expense of both people and natural resources. We are reclaiming our stories so that they are not used to support racist and classist thinking and institutions. And in the process, we are building a dynamic and politically engaged community of people of color with wealth to support each other in the work for the long haul.

Thinking about how and where to give, trying to get my money story straight, and talking frankly and openly about racism in my life or the ways in which I act out my class privilege have been truly beautiful struggles for me. And it's been totally worth it.

It has helped tremendously to have the support of a community of people of color with wealth by my side. Over the years, we encouraged each other to talk openly about our vision for change, we challenged each other to dig deeper into our personal narratives, we asked each other to give bigger, and we constantly reminded each other of how much more is possible when we work together. The support of this community has been my best cure for political uncertainty, burnout, fear of next steps, and a number of other challenges. So remember—you don't have to do this alone! We've been working hard to build a community and we can't wait to welcome you in.

Our work is a long-term commitment—it requires a lifetime of dedication. We are making an open declaration that we will do our part to fight for a better, more equitable world. No, it's not "cool" to be this openly idealistic. When we share our vision with others we run the risk of being dismissed as youthful and naive or told that we don't truly understand the world around us.

To these claims, I say: *OK.*

Call us idealistic because we care. Call us naive because we organize. Say we don't understand the world because we believe in community building. We are idealistic. We are hopeful. We do understand the world, which is exactly why we are working to change it. These are our best traits, and they are exactly the sentiments we need to take action. We can't do much without really believing that what we want is possible. We take the risk because we have a vision for a better world and we care deeply about it.

ALEXA'S COMMITMENT

" *When I starting working at the Global Fund for Women, I wanted to understand what it meant to have money and what I was supposed to do with it. It felt like I had more than my fair share.*

The Global Fund wasn't just about supporting direct service organizations. It wrestled with the question of redistributing wealth. How do we ensure that the leadership of the organization to which we're redistributing this money is run by the people that are most marginalized? Or, that the work that is being done is both for and by the people doing it? What is a strategic way to start to undermine systems of oppression that exist? What does it look like to pool my money with other individuals, whether it's large amounts or small? What does it mean for all of us to pool our money together?

These questions were really important. I wanted to figure out how to give my money away, how to shift systems, instead of only making loans to friends in need.

So, consider this an open invitation to bring everything you care about into social change work.

Bring the hope, the idealism, the righteous indignation, the outrage, the sense of justice.

This is the space to live out these big and wonderful visions.

So get out there!
You can do this!
Really.
Join us!

Bibliography.

Alexander, Michelle. *The New Jim Crow: Mass Incarceration in the Age of Colorblindness.* New York: New Press, 2010. Print.

Baldwin, James. *The Price of the Ticket: Collected Non-fiction, 1948–1985.* New York: St. Martin's Press, 1985. Print.

Collins, Chuck, and Felice Yeskel with United For a Fair Economy and Class Action. *Economic Apartheid in America: A Primer on Economic Inequality & Insecurity.* New York: New Press, 2005. Print.

Goldberg, Alison, Karen Pittelman, and Resource Generation. *Creating Change Through Family Philanthropy: The Next Generation.* Berkeley: Soft Skull Press, 2007. Print.

hooks, bell. *Killing Rage: Ending Racism.* New York: Henry Holt, 1995. Print.

hooks, bell. *Where We Stand: Class Matters.* New York: Routledge, 2000. Print.

Incite! Women of Color Against Violence. *The Revolution Will Not Be Funded: Beyond the Non-profit Industrial Complex.* Cambridge, MA: South End Press, 2007. Print.

Johnson, Allan G. *Privilege, Power, and Difference.* Columbus: McGraw-Hill, 2005. Print.

Lui, Meizhu, Barbara Robles, Betsy Leondar-Wright, Rose Brewer, and Rebecca Adamson, with United for a Fair Economy. *The Color of Wealth: The Story Behind the U.S. Racial Wealth Divide.* New York: New Press, 2006. Print.

Oliver, Melvin L., and Thomas M. Shapiro. *Black Wealth/White Wealth: A New Perspective on Racial Inequality.* New York: Routledge, 2006. Print.

Pittelman, Karen, and Resource Generation. *Classified: How to Stop Hiding Your Privilege and Use It for Social Change.* Berkeley: Soft Skull Press, 2005.

Wilkerson, Isabel. *The Warmth of Other Suns: The Epic Story of America's Great Migration.* New York: Random House, 2010. Print.

NICOLE LEWIS

Nicole's political development began with a simple question: What in the world is going on here? Growing up in Washington, DC, she was baffled by the seemingly contradictory intersection of racism and class privilege. In an attempt to make sense of things, she began attending and facilitating dialogue retreats while still in high school. In college, she continued to facilitate conversations with her peers focused on race and class, which eventually brought her to Resource Generation. Currently, Nicole is still perplexed by this world, but there are two things she knows for sure: The personal will always be political and a great conversation, like a great book, is the root of all understanding. When not trying to make sense of it all, Nicole spends her time laughing with friends or whipping up some deliciousness in her tiny Brooklyn kitchen. She holds a BA in English Literature with a minor in Women's Studies from the University of Michigan.

RESOURCE GENERATION organizes young people with financial wealth to leverage resources and privilege for social change. Since 1998, Resource Generation (RG) has engaged over 2,100 young people with wealth across the US. Through community building, education, and organizing, we help young people with wealth bring all they have and all they are to the social change movements and issues they care about. We organize to transform philanthropy, policy, and institutions, and leverage our collective power to make lasting structural change.

6083242R00039

Made in the USA
San Bernardino, CA
30 November 2013